TOUCHED

BY

GOD

TOUCHED

BY

GOD

Albert Edward Schueller

Touched by God
Published by Gatekeeper Press
2167 Stringtown Rd, Suite 109
Columbus, OH 43123-2989
www.GatekeeperPress.com

Library of Congress Control Number: 2021949758

ISBN (paperback): 9781662916502
eISBN: 9781662916519

Contents

Dedicated to Pastor Chris Davis, who saved my life.

Touched by God is the testimony of my direct encounter with God's boundless love. This is the testimony of my personal encounter with our Creator, who told me to write this and put my observations about His church down for consideration. I'm told I've been given time, but I must not waste it. I do not know how long I've been given, so I will do my best to make this testimony make sense.

In this modern world, humanity tends to view God's direct interactions with humanity as being in the remote past during biblical times. Nothing could be further from the truth. He is here now and is an active God, ready to become part of all of our lives in the present. My experience shows that miracles do happen, and they happen today.

My personal experience may be a little more overt, but we are surrounded by small miracles every day. Sometimes we fail to notice them, which does not mean they are not occurring; it is just that our expectations and perceptions in this life are colored by our earthly experiences, which are ones of skepticism and disbelief. We want proof somehow, as if you could find an earthly reason for the miracle. Of course, if you look hard enough for a reason for disbelief, eventually it will emerge.

This is the nature of the work of the evil one. Disbelief is his most effective weapon against humanity, and he works hard at providing us with reason for doubt. If you see a reason for belief, even a small miracle, embrace that and give thanks to God for allowing you to witness His love for us in action in the present. He truly surrounds us with miracles on a daily basis; we just need to have eyes that see clearly, so that we don't miss out on the joy that He provides to us.

I grew up in a large Catholic family. We learned the rites, the doctrine of the church, and multiple sacraments. Not to say that it was wrong, but for me, it was really just words and did not bring me to faith. I was sleepwalking through life. I eventually met my wife, who is a practicing Christian, and we decided that going to church would be part of our lives. We found a new church, which was nondenominational.

Unfortunately, the church turned out to be one where the emphasis was on judgment and not on loving kindness. I witnessed a public shaming during a service that set my search for faith back, and because of it, we left that church, and we were led to the man who restored my faith in a loving God. We hear of the happy warrior, and that is who my Pastor Chris was. Not just happy to be out sharing God's love, he was beyond happy; he was positively giddy with joy, and it was so apparent that I also wanted that. He set my feet on the path that I followed.

About ten years after we joined the church, we all got the news that Chris had been stricken by a brain cancer, one that was aggressive and not likely to be curable. Effective prayer does not have to be done in a quiet place all alone, but that certainly is a good strategy to avoid distractions when you're talking to God. In my case, my prayer was said sitting at a traffic light; pretty mundane. As I sat there thinking about Chris not seeing his small children grow up, I sobbed, and I prayed. "Please let me carry Chris's burden, and please give him some of my time here on Earth so that he can have the joy of seeing his children grow up."

Even though my faith in prayer at the time was weak, Jesus saw my pain and brought my prayer to God. And my prayer must have been in line with God's will for Chris, for He answered my prayer. This body I wear around this planet is going to die from the same type of brain cancer that afflicted Chris. I am full of joy and at peace with that, because this body was going to die eventually anyway. We all know it's going to happen, and we spend our lives preparing for the day, some in fear, some in hope. In answering my prayer, God put the cancer in me and touched me directly. Like Saul on the road to Damascus, my earthly body wasn't up to absorbing that much power, even though that power was God's love.

I spent a week in the hospital after that. When you wake up in the hospital, you are supposed to be fearful and confused, but I never experienced that. I woke up filled with joy, and was so happy I barely could contain myself. My wife was somewhat perplexed by my disposition. It was frankly hard to explain to her what had happened to me. To feel God's raw power of love was like trying to get a sip of water out of a fire hose; it nearly took my head off. It did overwhelm me, hence the hospitalization.

As a man of previously unexamined faith, I ask myself, why me? I don't know. All I do know is that God is great and gives His gifts freely, even to those of us who don't deserve it. Christ stands for those of us who are weak (all of us), and His love is gentle and will fill us at a pace that will keep us out of the hospital. It's all free for the asking. We don't even have to reach all the way; Jesus will reach back to us.

God wants us all—everyone on this big, beautiful planet. God created everything for a reason, that reason being that we help each other on this earth and seek out and bring people into a personal relationship with Christ. There is not any other purpose for life. We are here to seek God, as He seeks us.

When I was in the hospital, God sent me a dream. I was standing in a broad valley filled with people with heads bowed, ready to hear. Surrounding the valley, in the mountains, was a bright band encircling everything. But there was a problem; the field was ready for harvest, but the few harvesters available were not doing anything. They couldn't, because they had thrown away their only effective tool. I knew that God wanted that harvest, but without an effective tool, you cannot harvest a vast field, grain by grain, of your choosing.

The harvesters had thrown out Christ's love. We have in Christ the perfect teacher, who is unambiguous in His instruction. And in Christ's love we have the perfect tool to reap God's chosen. We just need to pick it up and use it, but this world is suffering a plague of men who purport to interpret His teaching, as if that needs to be done, deeming some of the people as unfit because of their sin.

We all sin. I can't stop sinning for thirty seconds at a time myself. It is our nature, and Jesus knows this and has already determined that we are His, even when we are not worthy, not one of us. For we weak and flawed mortals to determine someone isn't worthy of God's salvation because we don't like a person's sin is obviously at odds with God's will. We are okay with our sin, just not someone else's sin. To make this judgment, which many false teachers are using modern technology to spread, is causing some of God's chosen to drive away the very people that God wants so badly to have.

Jesus in His ministry reached the unclean, marginalized, and those which we erroneously call the dregs of society. Yet because of a lack of love for our fellow man, we don't follow Jesus's example and reach out to these people. To cause a person to not seek God because of our hatefulness or prejudice causes that person to determine our hope is false and makes an individual think there is nothing true to our message of redemption and salvation through Christ. Because we, who should be a perfect reflection of God's love, are actually projecting onto the person, when we should only be showing Christ's pure love, because God wants everyone, not only those we ourselves deem worthy.

1. Ready for the Harvest

We all are steeped in sin, and yet, Christ still finds us to be worthy. If you follow the second dictate of the greatest commandment to do unto others as you would have others do unto you, (Matthew 22:39) most of the trouble in this world would be far along toward the day where God's harvest can be reaped. When we help a new soul find God through Christ, we not only please God and further His desire to reap His harvest; we gain another reaper to help.

Jesus gave us a perfect prayer when He lived among us: "Our Father who art in heaven, Hallowed be thy name. Thy kingdom come, Thy will be done, On earth as it is in heaven. Give us this day our daily bread, And forgive us our debts, As we also have forgiven our debtors; And lead us not into temptation, But deliver us from evil." Matthew 6:9-13. Amen. When we pray this prayer, we are asking Jesus to forgive us in the manner we forgive our brothers and sisters here on Earth. We need to forgive others around us if they give offense, in loving kindness always, because we ask Christ to use that standard when He forgives us our sins.

Ask Jesus for a forgiving and loving heart always, one that is not only ready to forgive but is eager to forgive, as is Christ. In forgiveness is joy, and the burden of anger and hurt is removed from your life. This life is hard at times, of course, and hurt happens, but with Jesus, it does not have to be that way. He gives us perfect freedom from having to carry those burdens, which are just distractions from what we all should be focusing on, which is how to always be reconciled with one another.

Through the love of Christ, we pray that God transforms this world to be more like His heavenly abode, where we can have abounding love for each other. And what we ask, God provides us with our daily needs. He always does, because He made each and every one of us available to help each other meet those needs—not wants, but needs.

It is up to us to fulfill God's wish that we take care of each other in this world so no one suffers from want, and by that suffering of wants, fails to see the promise of salvation being offered as a free gift. It is hard to see the eternal when the mortal is under stress and need. Because, after all, we experience this world as mortals, and we all have actual earthly needs in order for the body to endure.

James 2:16 says, What good is it to tell someone to be fed and warmly dressed unless we by our actions make sure that happens. It is our calling to not only seek out those Christ wants, but to make sure that the multitudes are taken care of in their earthly needs, so when the call comes, they will be able to hear it over the distractions of their earthly needs, and be ready for the approaching judgment.

2. Approaching Judgment

Jesus, in His perfect Word, tells us His heart. In Matthew 25, His priorities for our treatment of our fellows is not hidden, but perfectly clear, and His judgment is also perfectly clear for those who fail to heed His words. Beware the false teachers plaguing this world who would have you deviate from the perfect Word that Jesus already has given us. Listen to our Lord Jesus only, and if any try to lead you aside, say, "Be gone, evil one," and pray Christ's deliverance from evil. We are to feed and clothe our brothers, welcome strangers, take care of the sick, visit the prisoners, and treat the least among us as we would like to be treated. It is hardly complicated as instructions go, but it does require some changes of heart for some people. Part of being able to take care of our fellows here on Earth will require work on our part to protect the world.

3. Protecting Our World

God gave us a beautiful, bountiful planet to be stewards over. It's God's planet. It is our job to protect it so that it can provide for all of our needs, as is His will. We do not own this planet, and treating it like a commodity to be used and destroyed for profit for the few does not please God. We all only have this one place of refuge in the universe, and we do have the ability to damage it beyond its ability to provide everyone's needs as God intended.

God has freely given everything we need to make the earth abundant enough to feed and house all His people, but we have to be caretakers of His gift, lest it lose that abundance. We need to make choices that will help preserve God's great and good planet to be home for all of God's people, wherever they live.

We have the know-how to have an industrial society without burning fossil fuels, but it will cost more, which means that certain segments of society will not be able to reap enormous profits. They already are objecting about how alternative energy sources are evil and expensive, so of course these memes are repeated by the captives of the very wealthy in the media, making it very hard to create a real program to make solar and wind power a viable alternative to fossil fuels. But, if we do not change soon to these alternatives, it may be too late to change the trajectory of Earth that is going to make the planet uninhabitable in the not-too-distant future. Sadly, this situation is the result of seeking excesses of earthly wealth.

4. The Danger of Wealth

Jesus said it's easier to pass a camel through the eye of a needle than a rich man through the gates of heaven. (Matthew19:24). In His mercy, God has cursed few of us with great wealth. All praise to God for that, because it's our sinful nature to love money and admire those who have way too much of it.

The problem isn't the money, but rather the obsession in getting more. A few men of great wealth have discovered that the best way to deal with the problem is to give it away as fast as possible, or to use it constructively to help solve the world's problems by finding cures to disease, better ways to feed the hungry, and ways to improve the lives of their fellow men. This is pleasing to God, as it conforms to His will that we care for each other. But not all of us are strong enough to be able to give all of our earthly possessions away. God knows we are weak, so He does not tempt most of us with that kind of wealth. God does provide most of us with an abundance of blessings, which He expects we will share with those in need. We live in a society where we collectively are allowed to determine how to share that abundance that God provides.

5. God's Provisioning of All Our Needs

God has provided more than enough for everyone, if only we share that provisioning. We have elections where we get to freely choose to share our blessings with others. When we see proposals to raise taxes on ourselves to help those in need or to help the planet that we all share, we should always say, "Yes. Please raise my taxes so that collectively we can do God's bidding in making the lives of everyone better here until the day Christ returns in all His glory."

Sadly, I have heard people who say they are Christians say, "I just don't like to see people get free stuff," as if we are not the recipients of more free stuff than we can count. We receive eternal life free for the asking, forgiveness of our transgressions for free, a whole planet to live on for free. We didn't make the earth or the sun; it is all free, as are our very earthly lives. We didn't earn or work for them; all are free gifts from God.

God's very love is His free gift to us all. Not liking to see people get free stuff indicates a heart that thinks it is better than its fellows and somehow has earned what has been given by God to us freely, which is arrogant and false, as no one has earned what God has provided us. It is only through God's generosity that any of us have anything, even our very earthly lives. Not wanting to share our material wealth to make this a better place for everyone is not pleasing to God.

The widow's story in Mark demonstrates the attitude of giving that is pleasing to God. It is not the amount given but the spirit in which it is given that counts. If you cannot give freely like the poor widow, don't bother to give, as what is given begrudgingly will be counted as sin against you. It shows God a heart that loves earthly possessions more than one's fellow man.

Paul writes correctly, of course, in Ephesians 2:8, that, "It is by grace we have been saved, through faith," while James writes in 2:18, "Show me your faith without deeds, and I will show you my faith by what I do." Both are correct. It is by God's grace that we are saved through faith. Another free gift. James is saying that true faith will express itself through doing God's will here on Earth, through good works, demonstrating loving kindness to others and acts of faith.

Once God's love is in you, there will be no stopping you in your efforts to please Him with your actions here on Earth. Your faith in God's undying love will compel you to do His will here on Earth. It is the greatest unstoppable force in existence and available to us all for the asking. Just ask God to draw close, and Jesus will bridge any gap for you, and God will embrace you as a new son or daughter. It is a wonder beyond comprehension for our feeble human selves, but it is true; God wants all of us to be with Him for eternity and is willing to bridge that gap. All we need do is ask, and we will receive.

6. God's Embrace Here on Earth

God gives us this life here on Earth as a pale preview of what to expect in our heavenly home. This life is a gift from God; He wants us to live it here, so we must. Live your life with your eyes wide open. God's creation cries out His greatness everywhere you look; we just need to open our eyes and appreciate it all like new babies.

Everything is new and fresh to a baby. We become jaded in our day-to-day living, and life slides by without our really seeing God's greatness surrounding us. Life here is God's gift, and He means for us to enjoy His gift in full. Open your eyes and really see His creation. Savor each moment as the gift it is. Stop and give praise often, and be mindful of the goodness and love God put into His earthly creation. This life is not a challenge to overcome but a gift to enjoy, and we should absolutely enjoy the bounty God has given us.

Life is meant to be a preview of the perfect to come. So, in this world, God does want us to enjoy and appreciate His abundant bounty, but in a way that is always aware of how good and loving He is to us all. Stop often and thank God for the little things that might escape notice. It all cries out to us if we will only see and listen. Stop, see, smell, feel, and praise always.

God gave us these bodies to wear here on Earth to experience life, and it is His will that we enjoy His gift. The only thing God asks is that we treat this life as the precious gift it is. By all means, if you enjoy an activity, take part; just make sure that that pleasure does not become the focus of your life, for the danger is to lose sight of God in the process. Enjoy life, all the while praising God for giving you the opportunity to enjoy and experience goodness here in life.

These bodies we wear are greedy, always seeming to want more. Overindulgence in life's pleasures means that we really don't experience the fullness of the gift God gives us. We become sated and miss how good and special the thing is. A small taste of an exquisite pastry is much better than the whole thing, because our senses are more attuned to appreciate that small taste rather than being overwhelmed by the whole thing.

If we approach God's gifts in anticipation, ready to appreciate them and fully experience them, our praise and thankfulness will flow out to God's ear and greatly please Him. This is a world full of troubles that cannot be avoided, so it is through focusing on God's goodness and all the small perfections He surrounds us with that we avoid letting the cares of this world overwhelm us.

7. God's Caretakers of Each Other

The cure for the problem of the world's ills overwhelming us is to always keep our eyes firmly fixed on our God's greatness. He has us all in His hands, and we do not need to worry. We do need to care, though, as we are His caretakers here and need to do His work to make this world more like His kingdom to come. We will fall far short of that, but we can make this into a good and loving world if we follow the True Word. We must love each other as Christ loves us and treat others not just as we would like to be treated, but treat them as the Lord treats us, as precious and worthy things to be cherished and treasured.

We have no greater purpose in this world than helping each other through this earthly life. So, every person can experience God's creation and learn to see God's power and love in everything He has created.

It is hard for people to appreciate God's bounty if in their lives there is want, hunger, or lack. We must be God's agents in making sure that every person's basic needs here on Earth are provided for. Christ, in Matthew 25, tells us exactly what God wants us to do, and His words should strike fear in the hearts of those who do not follow His perfect instruction. Heed God's warning. We have no excuses if we fail to obey God's will. Jesus is not only clear as to what God wants; He is clear what the consequences of failure on our part are.

Our loving God sent a perfect teacher to us so that we would know what our Creator wants most of us. We are to be a reflection of His love to the world. We need to become beacons reflecting His love and light in order to be effective emissaries to the world.

8. Christ's Light

We are not the light, but God's light reflects from us if we live in His Word given to us by His perfect teacher, Christ. Our faith in God's love and salvation should pour forth from us and thus should show the world a giddy joy that we cannot contain, showing such an abundance of love that we cannot help but spread it to everything and everyone that we come across.

How can we reach the world unless the world wants what we so obviously have? Too many of us hide that light under a basket because we don't want to appear foolish. We need to be foolish for Christ. Show the light, and be a beacon of hope for the world. The broken Earth needs God's light and the good news of eternal life we have to share. So, be foolish in your love so that God's harvest can be brought in before God determines the time has arrived for the reaping.

God wants His harvest brought in, and it is through Christ's love we reach the world. Be ecstatic in your love and joy, and we will be able to reach all the world with the active help of Christ. Our part is to convince the world to seek God out, and Christ will reach across any gap for them. They belong to Him, and He wants them. Beware of your own sin.

9. Sin and Judgment

All true Christians know what sin is because we recognize we all are hopeless sinners. Sometimes we somehow rationalize that our sin is okay, but the sin of a fellow is worse than ours, even when we know that is not true. What is shown to the world is judgment that they are not somehow worthy of God's saving love.

Jesus tells us to take the plank out of our own eye before worrying about the speck in our neighbor's eye. We are in no position to make any judgment about our fellows' sins; that is the province of Christ alone. We need to stop being the reason people stop seeking God's salvation because of our sin and judgment.

The teacher gives us the tools we need to get out of His way. In love, there is no judgment, but there is a realization that we all are in the same situation. In an imperfect world, under attack from the evil one, embrace your brothers and sisters in sin in loving kindness because you, too, are a sinner. Ask for Jesus's forgiveness for your failures. Christ's clear instruction in John 13:34 is to "love one another as I have loved you," which is unconditional, even knowing that we are not worthy of that love and still full of sin. He loves us anyway.

Let the Love of Christ well out of you so that it is all the world sees. His good news should be all we reflect. "God loves you and wants you at His side for eternity" is all we should be demonstrating to those who God so wants. We are all created in God's image.

God being spirit makes us also spiritual in nature. These bodies we experience the world in are not to be mistaken for God's image but are the very temporary abodes for the spirit that the Creator has provided us with to live in this world. We, of course, have experienced all that we know from the perspective of these earthly bodies, so it is not surprising that many make the mistake of thinking that this life is real life, when nothing could be farther from the truth.

God, out of His great love for us, has created a reality for all of us to experience for eternity with Him. While we are here on Earth, in these bodies, God will send tests and trials for us to overcome. It is our challenge to rise to the occasion and resist as best we can, always fully asking in prayer for Christ's aid to surmount our trials. Fear for the end of our bodies, of death, is natural to anyone who is not connected to God, which makes it even more imperative that those of us who already have accepted God's free gift of life demonstrate that great and boundless love to everyone.

10. Welcome the Stranger

This divided and broken world needs all brothers and sisters in faith to be vocal in their love for all. Unfortunately, this is not always the case. God instructs us to work with our hands for our living here on Earth and to seek to live a quiet and humble life. We are in a time where many are seeking to follow God's very edict, but who are being persecuted for trying to follow God's will.

The problem is not the people seeking to follow God's will, but those who fail to welcome the stranger who may have another language and may follow different cultural cues, but is also God's chosen. How can we ignore Jesus's instructions in Matthew 25? "I was a stranger and you invited me in."

Jesus makes it very clear what our Creator wants us to do. This rejection of God's instruction is especially offensive to God because the stranger is just seeking to do what God instructs us all to do: work with our hands and seek to live a modest and humble life.

The Earth is currently undergoing changes that are going to make living here in our mortal bodies more difficult. So, there will be many more opportunities to welcome strangers as they flee their current homes, which will become barren and unfruitful. We must be a place of refuge for these brothers and sisters in their time of need. To fail in that is to bring God's judgment against ourselves.

Jesus tells in His perfect Word and perfect truth that whatever we do for the least of these, we do to Christ Himself. They may be the least of these to us, but Jesus equates their worth as far higher than many who claim His name. Listen to our Christ: take the stone out of your heart, so that you can see clearly His desire that you reflect His love in a pure and worthy manner, to seek to feed those in need, welcome those who are strangers, and give drink and clothing to those who are in need.

Christ will separate us into those who follow His true Word, as those who ascend to heaven to be with God for eternity, and those who choose to live by this corrupt world's standards to be judged and cast down, to be separated from Christ and suffer the punishment He deems worthy for eternity.

Don't be on Christ's left side on that day of judgment. Examine your hearts, brothers and sisters in Christ, and let Christ's pure love guide your path here in this broken world so that when God's hour arrives, you are ready for our Lord to examine your heart and see only what is pleasing to Him. In seeing your heart, He will grant you eternal life in our eternal and perfect refuge.

11. Worry

One area where the evil one can insert his tendrils into your life is through worry. Many people living in this broken world are consumed by worry. What does the future hold? Worry is based on fear of the future. As Christian brothers and sisters, we know we are in God's hands completely. It is all under our Creator's divine plan. When we worry, we not only tell God we have a lack of faith in His boundless love for us, but it takes time from the present, which we could be using to sing His praises and appreciate His creation in its fullest. We, after all, live in the present, and worry is about a time in the future that we cannot experience. Here on Earth, we can only experience the present.

We rob ourselves of God's precious gift of the present when we worry. God very much wants us to experience the present in its fullest in order to sing God's praises concerning His abundant provision of His wonderful creation. If you worry, ask God's forgiveness for your lack of trust, and ask for Jesus to intercede and strengthen your faith and trust in an all-loving and powerful God. Jesus is always ready to step in to lend you His strength to stop your worries from becoming a focus of anxiety.

There is nothing worth being anxious about in this world. Experience shows most people that their anxieties turn out to be overblown in retrospect, not worth the time they robbed themselves of in the worry and anxiety. It is trusting God, and sometimes those around you, that is key to turning aside the evil one's assault on your peace and joy.

If you worry, Jesus is always your answer. Ask, and He will give you peace of mind and remind you of God's abounding love and protection. The evil one is the source of our worries in order to drive a wedge between God and us. Always be mindful that it is his aim to break the bond of love and trust between our Creator and us. Pray Christ's protection from the evil one whenever you start feeling worry and anxiety.

As brothers or sisters in Christ, it is imperative that we recognize the assault and immediately call out to Jesus for protection so that the evil one's intent does not overwhelm us, for in Christ we have strength beyond anything we can marshal on our own. His strength is greater than that of the evil one. Sometimes our worry is about keeping our worldly possessions safe from others.

12. Gun Culture and Hunting

Somehow, in the modern era, gun culture and Christian culture are bizarrely intertwined. How we leap from the pure love of Christ to that of a love of weapons is beyond comprehension. There are legitimate uses for these tools—recreation such as target shooting, which is an acceptable activity that God created for us to enjoy in this life, and hunting for food to sustain these earthly bodies. If you enjoy hunting, by all means, target shoot so as to be proficient and skillful in your hunting, so that when God offers up one of His creations for harvest, you end its existence in a clean and humane way. Always be mindful that, for the animal, this really is the end of its life. It is God who provided you with the opportunity to harvest it for your use. Don't waste what God provides, but use it to feed yourself and family and friends, as is God's intent.

The senseless killing of living things, however, is offensive to God. God's creatures were created by Him to live in this world with us. They are not targets, but living creatures imbued with life by the same God that gives us life. They, however, do not have a second life in paradise such as we do. So, the life they have now is all they will have, and we must take care to not cause the needless loss of a life God created.

If you hunt and God grants you one of His creatures to harvest, do enjoy the gift that God gives you. Some people want to mount a display of the successful hunt. This is fine as long as the mount or cape displayed is for the purpose of remembering the gift given.

Trophy hunting is truly offensive to God. God didn't create life in these creatures just to satisfy the vanity of shallow men who do not actually hunt the animal but are driven up to the poor beast, at which point the "hunter" pulls out a rifle and kills the animal in cold blood. Then, the "hunter" poses with his crime victim in some sort of perverse celebration of the act of killing one of God's creations for no greater need than to feed one's vanity and emptiness. This also reveals a coward's heart.

If you need to trophy hunt, then hunt, do not just kill. Examine the reason that you are doing the hunt. If it is for vanity or ego, it is ungodly, but if it is to use the experience as a test of skills with the aim of using God's gift fully, not wasting an animal's life, then it is in God's will.

It's argued that trophy hunting is necessary in order for us humans to maintain the population of those animals subject to the activity. That is not true. We humans need to share space with God's created animals. Mostly, it is loss of habitat, a simple place to live, that is driving down the numbers of animals we share the planet with. We humans are greedy and want all the land, leaving little for God's animals. The solution is for us to set aside good, fruitful land for the use of the animals, and God will watch over them and their increase in numbers, as is His will.

It is our duty as God's caretakers of this world to ensure that the animals are protected in their homes from evil men who would kill them for a bit of horn, ivory, or other body part. God's intent for His creatures is that they share our earthly home with us and abound. They need our help for this to happen, and it's God's will that we provide the help. Hunting fees from trophy hunting are used for this purpose, but there is a way to provide monies for preservation without depending on the destruction of one of God's wonderful creations. But those solutions cost money, which some value above God's creations.

Other than hunting or recreation, there is an evil reason to have weapons. Jesus instructs us that if someone takes your cloak, give him your shirt. Having weapons in order to protect your possessions is truly a sign that the Word is not with you. Nothing you might have on this earth is as valuable as a single human life, and to have weapons to make sure that no one takes your stuff is abhorrent to God. After all, it is God who gave you these earthly possessions you so worry about. To be willing to kill another to prevent them from taking from you what is obviously of greater value to you than their life is against God's will.

A more godly path exists. If you value your stuff so highly, it is more in line for you to give it away so that possessions do not corrupt your relationship with God. If someone comes to take your possessions, greet them and give them what they need, rather than fight for worthless trash, which it is if it is what is keeping you from connecting with your Lord and Savior.

In killing someone over your worthless earthly trash, you could end the life of someone not yet ready to hear the call of God. That person, given more time here in this life, could become in time your brother or sister in Christ and also get the free gift of eternal life that God wants the person to enjoy with Him in eternity.

It's a winning solution when we follow Jesus's instruction to give our possessions away. We lose that which is holding us back from God, and the person doing the potential receiving sees the love of our Lord shining through and will be open to God's embrace. We gain a brother or sister in Christ and also another to help with the vast harvest we need to get in for the greater glory of God.

There are evil men loose in the world who would do us harm. These men have only the power to kill our earthly bodies and cannot kill our true selves. Only God has that power. But we want to protect ourselves from them with weapons in this life. A medium-sized vocal dog is much more likely to be of protection to you and your family than a gun will ever be, and you get the advantage of enjoying one of God's small miracles. The love and devotion for us that God built into the dogs He provided us on Earth is a concrete example of unquestioning love and devotion, one which we would be well served to emulate in our search for those seeking out Christ.

The other problem with guns in the home is that the gun in the home is more likely to end the life of its owner or family members of the owner due to an accident or a failure of the owner to secure the gun, or during moments of despair in this life, to readily seek the comfort of Christ.

Life can look pretty bleak here on Earth at times, and even believers can fall into moments of weak faith. After all, we are all under assault from the evil one, and he is far cleverer than we are. He can affect our thinking for a time while we pray for Christ's strength. But a gun makes a rash decision to end it all here on Earth too easily attainable while we are not in our right mind with Christ.

Guns were invented for one purpose only, the taking of life, and they are very effective at it. They are earthly tools made to solve perceived earthly problems. As children of God, brothers and sisters in Christ, examine yourself and make sure your reason for having a gun is in keeping with God's allowed reasons for having that tool around you in all things. Also, seek out Christ to counsel you on your search for answers. He will guide you in loving kindness to make correct and godly decisions that are pleasing to your Creator. As always, it is your choice.

13. Choice

We are all created in the image of God, and God being spirit, this means that we are also spirit created by God from ancient days. We live in a very broken world, where people choose to be divided one from the other over issues that should bring unity, yet we choose to be divided due to our failure to follow the Lord's true Word.

God created man with free will so that man could choose his path freely. It is up to us all to choose to follow a path that brings honor and praise to God. The creation of a new mortal life has become an area rife with conflict in our broken world. This need not be.

The vessel that God creates when He brings a new mortal body into the world is a wonderful thing, but we have been separated into two camps, pro-choice and pro-life, when in actuality both camps are working toward the same ends, that is, fewer abortions. The pro-choice faction encourages taking care of the basic needs of the poor and their children, so when the time comes for a free-will choice by the mother, the choice she will make is yes, have the baby. The pro-life (pro-birth) side has sadly been hijacked by politicians using the division to keep hold of political power and working to make the division worse than it needs to be.

Pro-choice is not the same as pro-abortion. Pro-choice wants the options available to the mother to meet the basic needs of the child so that when the time comes to choose, she will choose to have the baby. If the pro-life faction wants to make a difference, they can work toward taking care of the baby after birth. Both sides can work together to meet the needs of the child; hence all mothers will want to have their children.

14. Political Corruption

Political corruption is displeasing to God. Self-serving politicians use the pro-life/pro-choice divide as an issue of the day to further their own political influence and wealth, while deliberately failing to work for the greater good of the people who most need help.

Sadly, most of them self-identify as Christians, leading many brothers and sisters in Christ to be deceived as to their true purpose, which is to further their earthly influence rather than the work Christ sent them to accomplish. If a politician *must* identify himself or herself as a Christian, he or she is almost certainly not a true follower of Christ. If politicians are true followers, their love and good works flow out of them, leaving no question of their devotion to God's love and desire to please God in all their work. Instead, we have these supposed lovers of God and Christ doing things like cutting health care for the needy, cutting back programs to feed children, and also claiming there is no money to pay for the programs, while at the same time giving away more money to tax cuts for the already obscenely wealthy. They are also preventing workplace fairness rules and refusing to raise the minimum wages of the working poor, all in the corrupt seeking of money from the very wealthy people who are their real constituents.

It is pure corruption, as is the unholy relationship of church and state. That is, religious leaders giving credence to the corrupt politicians, and the politicians corrupting the religious leaders with access to political influence, which is what some so-called leaders are actually after, seeking earthly influence. Take note: it is this failure by our political leaders in ensuring the basic needs of the working poor that is a cause of abortions by not providing for the least among us, as Jesus commands in Matthew 25. Stop complaining, and do your job already. Start following the true Word of our Lord Jesus.

There is a true evil loose in the world. Unfortunately, this scourge seems to be focused on one political party within this country. A party that is not working for God's ends but rather to further the ends of the rich and powerful of this earth. This is not pleasing to God, and His judgment on our country may be severe unless we all act in concert to bring an end to the corrupt and evil cycle.

As brothers and sisters in Christ, we must look closely at what these politicians actually do, rather than assume because they call themselves Christians that they are in fact followers of our true Lord. Such open defiance of God's will will be for Christ to judge on the final day. Woe unto them, since I have felt the touch of God's love directly, and the power in that was so overwhelming, I cannot even begin to comprehend what the touch of God's wrath will be like for these men who have abandoned God's love for earthly influence.

Brothers and sisters in Christ, I implore you to use your privilege of choosing our leaders to vote in such a way that true lovers of God and the Word are running our country in a way that conforms to God's will and so save not only our nation, but transform the entire country into a beacon for the entire broken world to look upon and draw hope from. It is within our grasp to accomplish this if we act following Christ's perfect Word and allow His love to dwell within us and to flow out for all the world to see. In Christ's perfect love, there is always hope that with His help, we can accomplish His purpose here on this earth.

We can all be part of the solution or choose to remain part of the problem if we ignore God's instructions to take care of each other. If you knowingly vote for politicians who pervert our government policies away from taking care of people, to take care of the wealthy or corporations, then you bear responsibility for the problem of abortion directly as you are not providing for your fellows as instructed by your Lord. You do not get a free pass on this issue; you are part of the problem.

15. The Death Penalty

The flip side of the pro-life movement is the movement to use the death penalty for certain crimes. The death penalty has been shown by statistics not to affect the crime rate, so why the push for its use? If it is for vengeance, this clearly is against God's stated will. "Vengeance is mine," saith the Lord in Romans 12:19. It does not get much clearer than that.

People who claim the mantle of pro-life cannot in good conscience be pro-death at the same time. There are dangerous people who need to be locked away in secure locations to protect society from their evil, so by all means, protect society and lock them away. But the death penalty is not the solution for evil people. It is by locking such individuals safely away that we protect ourselves.

Some people scoff at jailhouse conversions, where a convicted man or woman claims to come to Christ while in prison. What better place to come to Christ? People are faced with their crimes and cannot deny the wrong they have done, and they have time to reflect and seek to be forgiven by their Lord and Savior. Jesus, in Matthew 25, seems to have a special place in His heart for the prisoners, recognizing the extra support that these people need in order to be drawn to Him. If we use the death penalty, we of course cut short the possibility of such people ever being drawn to Christ as is God's intent. The correct and godly path is to keep society safe by sequestering dangerous people away safely, not by cutting their lives here on Earth short and possibly causing them to miss the call to eternal life when it is issued by Christ, who actively seeks us all out.

16. God Walking Among Us Today

Too many people living now view God as exalted and unapproachable, so far above us that He can't possibly be approached. I can attest from personal experience that God is walking among us in the modern age. He seeks us to draw near and for us to seek out His light.

We have Immanuel (God with us) always, in the form of our Lord Jesus, God's sent Messiah, who saves the whole world and who allows us to dare approach God in a direct and worshipful way. Through Christ we have a direct conduit to God's unbounding love and kindness. We have Jesus's assurance in the book of Matthew that He will be with us always directly, even unto the end of the age. He is here walking among us; we only have to ask, and He will act in our lives. That is His promise, and His promise is always true. Just remember to ask it in prayer.

17. Prayer

God will act today for any person who sincerely asks for His intercession, so pray your prayers to God in faith so that they conform to God's will for you. Don't insult God with selfish prayers, as He takes offense at selfish prayer. Pray only for that which will help ease the burdens of our fellow brothers and sisters. Pray prayers that strengthen your faith and prayers of thankfulness. He finds prayers we pray that are unselfish and out of an abundance of love to be pleasing, and if the prayer is in keeping with His purpose, He answers.

From personal experience, I can attest to the truth that prayer is answered. In this modern age, and even though my faith was weak, through Christ, I received the answer to my prayer. Thanks be to God always. I am blessed by God. I have been granted my prayer in the present and am being allowed to be used by Him for His purpose. It is an honor I did not earn and do not deserve. That God would grant me, a weak and broken man, this honor moves me to such joy that I cannot suppress constant tears of joy and thankfulness that I can be a tool for God, even in my current broken state.

I am finding this experience to be much moister than expected. I have tears of joy and thankfulness always. Our Lord provides us all ample reason to experience His love and joy in a way that will drive a boom in the tissue industry.

Pray always. God is out there, always waiting to hear from us, and He will also overfill you with love, peace, and joy. Give thanks always to our Creator and loving God for His generous provision of all the love and joy that are available to us with a simple request, made through Christ, who told us to just ask, and we will receive. This is certainly true, for He is the Word and the truth, sent from the Father to intercede on our behalf.

DO NOT delay in asking; He is walking among us today, and He wants to hear from you today. Now is the time to act. To delay in asking only causes you to miss out on the peace and joy that are yours for today. And it is God's desire that you receive His free gift today so you can live in this broken world and still be filled with hope and be His instrument to create the change that He desires for this world.

Without His hope and peace, our task is going to be nearly impossible. God wants to hear from you now, and we need to hear from God now in order to do His will here on Earth. Pray, brothers and sisters, for His will to be done here on Earth as in heaven. Such will be the case if your prayer is true, because then your heart will be willing to change in order to make come true on Earth His will, that we take care of each other as Christ Jesus would have us do and to cherish all of our brothers and sisters in Christ to the fullest.

18. Black Lives Matter

We live in a country that identifies itself as white and Christian. Both of these descriptions are false. This country is not a white country, nor by our actions do we have any right to claim Christ's mantle and proclaim His holy name when by our actions we prove that we are not His followers and we show the world the opposite of Jesus's truth.

Black Lives Matter is the collective cry of an oppressed class within our society. God wants us to heed their plea. Making the social media rounds today is the statement "All lives matter," which is a message meant to bring division between people. This emerged from within white supremacist circles. These things are said by brothers and sisters in Christ who are trying to justify their privilege within our society by telling the oppressed within the society to "just get over it." The "it" being hundreds of years of mistreatment by the larger society.

The persons stating "all lives matter" are not Christian people and have no right to claim Christ's holy name. By their statement, they make plain to all that they actually feel themselves to be somehow better than their non-European brothers and sisters.

If Jesus were to appear today in human form, many of His shallow followers would reject Him because He was born in the Middle

East, and today He would be identified as one of those people because of His appearance. The arts have always tended to portray Christ as a handsome man of European descent, which is certainly false. Abraham was from what is today Iraq, so he would be dark-skinned and brown-eyed with dark hair. Jesus, being Abraham's descendent, would Himself be of similar appearance.

Do we reject the Messiah because He does not conform to our prejudiced view of what we think He should look like? Isaiah 53 tells us clearly that Jesus's physical body when He trod the Earth during His ministry was not one that would draw people to Him because of His appearance, rather only because of His message of salvation and eternal life that He preached were His followers drawn to Him. If God saw fit to bring the salvation of the world and all mankind through what we would call a person of color, who are we to place a higher value on whiteness than the Lord God Creator of heaven and Earth and the entire universe?

The people who repeat "all lives matter" almost certainly never lie awake at night worrying that their sons or daughters will not be coming home because of what they look like. But they know that being part of the privileged class in society provides protection to their children. While knowing this, those who persist in minimizing the pain and suffering of the oppressed class will indeed be judged by Christ for their lack of love for God's people. He will ask them, "Why did you not work for justice for my people?" I hope you have a good answer ready for when Jesus asks His question, as there is no real answer other than, "I failed you, O Lord. Please forgive me my sin," which is what we all should be doing today, because, on the day of judgment, it will be too late to ask forgiveness for our hard heart and lack of action.

We need to be seeking social justice every day for the rest of our earthly lives. Failure to follow God's true Word brings condemnation upon those who fail to act, personally and as a part of larger society. Everyone else failing to act is not an excuse for you not to act. We can phone the people who are supposed to follow our wishes within government directly and make known to them where we stand on these issues. If enough of God's people call and inform them that social justice is a priority above making the wealthy even richer, then they will get the message that their grip on power might be lost, power being the only thing many of these so-called leaders are actually interested in.

Our collective actions will cause them to act faithfully, if only out of fear that they will lose their positions of privilege and power. God wants all of His chosen to benefit from lives that are fair and free of fear of oppression, and we as Christ's chosen are to be the instruments to ensure that the ideal becomes the reality. We may not be able to bring it to perfection on this evil Earth, but to fail to actively act to bring about God's will to bring a more just world will be counted against us on that final day.

As brothers and sisters in Christ, make your voice heard in order to bring about the changes that God wants us to make. The harvest that God wants us to reap is composed of vast numbers of people who do not look like you, yet these are the Lord's chosen. Do not fail the Creator in His pursuit of His chosen people. It is God's desire for the entire world that the principle of social justice be applied to all the earth's people and that we act in a way that allows all of Earth's people to equally receive the benefits of the current earth's bounty, which is not reserved for any one nation.

19. Dangers of Nationalism

Unfortunately, loose in the world are the ideas of nationalism and exceptionalism. It has been said, "My country, right or wrong." This has to be one of the most damaging slogans ever created. In saying it, people are actually saying that they have elevated their country to be above God Himself.

Is not "Have no other gods before me" God's first commandment, given to Moses by God Himself? It is your country, and you can love it, but if your country is not acting within the true Word, and you accept its actions, you are elevating it above God Himself and have created a false God to worship. It cannot go well with you or your country if you fail to act in a way that promotes God's agenda within your country. All praise to God if your country is on the path He seeks, but if it is not, and is in the wrong, then you cannot accept its actions, but must resist the wrong actions even if doing so puts you at odds with the authorities.

We are warned by Jesus that in the end times, these things will take place, and the elect will be persecuted for trying to bring about God's will here on Earth. So, be ready to face persecution and hardships in your quest to do God's bidding here on Earth. Persecution and hardships, even unto the death of your earthly bodies, are coming, so be ready to make a stand for God, and fear not for your earthly life, for it is but for a short time. In any case, it is through God that our true life is to be lived for eternity in paradise with all the people of true faith that God calls to Himself. We will live forever with our Creator, as was the plan from the very creation. If your country is wrong, it is your duty to God to try to correct the error.

In the Old Testament, there are numerous cases where Israel as a nation turned its back on the Lord and failed to follow His instructions, at which point God turned His back on Israel. If God turns His back on a nation, that nation is doomed. Take heed: God will also turn His back on our nation if our nation turns its back to God, with devastating effects.

Ours is only one nation under God so long as we have God's protection because we strive to do His work in this world, and God will bring about the humbling of any nation defiant to His will. This is assuredly going to happen if we as a people turn our back on God and cease to hear His true Word and follow His teachings. God wants our obedience to His wishes in order for our country to continue under His protection. Failure to be faithful will result in our country losing God's protection. A large part of how we honor God as a nation is through spending priorities.

20. Military Spending

Massive military spending by our nation is an offensive thing. We spend billions of dollars on weapons, yet somehow we cannot find the money to take care of those among us who need help finding enough to eat, having enough to wear, or locating a safe place to live. What are our priorities as a nation? Doing God's bidding or military dominance here on Earth? It would seem to be military dominance, rather than God's will. And, for this reason, God will turn His back on us, for we turned from Him first.

The massive military is primarily used to ensure that the nation's corporations are able to continue to operate in stripping the resources of this planet for their benefit, rather than for the good of all mankind, as is God's intent. We use our power to ensure our companies have an unfair competitive advantage for our planet's resources, which is for the benefit of the few who reap massive profits to add to their already obscene wealth.

How is it that we always have money for death and destruction but somehow never have enough to fulfill God's desire that we care for the least among us as commanded by God? Is this the face we as a nation want to show our God and Creator? The situation is only going to get worse as the planet's resources become scarcer and other powers use their militaries in the same manner we use ours. The race is on to steal what can be stolen from the collective needs of all the people who are currently living on this swiftly declining planet.

The aim of our purpose should not be taking what we want, but fulfilling God's desire that we share everything available equally with all the world's people so that when the time comes, there will be enough to go around for everyone, and no one suffers needlessly, and because of that suffering and earthly want, fails to hear God's call when it comes. As agents of God on Earth, it is our charge to ensure that the call is heard. God wants His harvest, and it is our duty to God to ensure that the world is provisioned in such a way that we all can hear God's call when it comes.

21. The Coming End

During His ministry here on Earth, Jesus foretold the times to come: a troubled time of famine, war, and rumor of war. The wars will be fought over the one thing that should be left just where it is: oil. God created this earth as Eden, and it is man in his quest for earthly wealth that has despoiled it to the point that it will have trouble feeding all of mankind. It is our duty as seekers after God's will that we work together with other nations to ensure that the damages we are inflicting on the planet cease, or all will be lost.

God gave us an abundant Earth, but we turned it into a garbage dump, polluting the planet from pole to pole, to the point that many of the creatures God created with the world cannot survive in the damaged wreck that we are leaving them. We can have famine and wars and untold horrors, or we can do God's bidding and work to ensure that the continued use of oil and coal, that is the main reason the planet's carbon cycle is getting so off-balance, stops. We must work with other nations to ensure that the current trends do not continue, for if we do not, our God's created Eden will no longer function.

To allow our government not to work with the rest of the world's nations to end this madness is offensive to God. To deny that which is so obviously happening is sin, and God will judge you according to the amount of damage your sin causes. The oceans will cease to provide their bounty first, then the land will begin to die. Must we wait until even the blindest cannot fail to see before we take actions that begin to slow the cycle of the destruction of our home? If we wait until the ocean dies, it will be too late to do anything but suffer through the cataclysmic end of this world.

God has shown man many other ways to power his economy, but we choose to use fossil fuels because it is cheaper and easier and allows for massive profits for the few over the needs of everyone else on the planet. The price we will all pay for the rampant greed of the few will be very high indeed. The danger is real, and so many of the world's poor and needy will be so adversely affected that they will not be able to feed their earthly bodies. God's harvest will be delayed because the people He is calling out for will be hearing their own empty stomachs instead of hearing His call. It is difficult to be dying of starvation here on Earth and to listen for God's call.

As believers in the Word, we must be the ones taking action. It is our leaders who are refusing to work with other nations to mitigate the damage we have done, so we must let those leaders know that they must start doing God's bidding before all is lost here on Earth. God gave us all we need here on Earth to prosper; it has been our choice to wreck the perfect planet He provided us. And now we have to face the future Jesus described during His ministry here on Earth.

The Word has spoken, and He is the true Word of God, so we can only pray that He has mercy on us and shortens those days so that we can try to take care of those of His harvest that are most in danger of being lost because of our carelessness and greed. God have mercy on us all.

When the time comes, the rich nations of the planet must share with the poor nations freely so that the harvest may be bought in. God will judge harshly those who try to hold onto what they have without feeding and caring for those afflicted during the coming famines. We as a nation can stop spending billions on our oversized military and instead use that money to feed the hungry, clothe the naked, and welcome the stranger as Jesus instructs us to do.

The time to choose is now. Do we want to be on Jesus's left or on His right? If you want to hear the words, "Well done, good and faithful servant," your instructions from God could not be more clear. Put aside your earthly comforts when the time comes to share, and make God's will the focus of your life. There are literally billions of souls still ready for harvest, and God wants them all, and it is up to the followers of Christ to ensure that they are reached before God decides that this world's time has come to pass away.

Time is short, and all of God's people must redouble their efforts and always pray that God grant us additional time to reap His harvest. Using Christ's perfect love and showing ourselves to be a reflection of God's perfect light, we can reach the world through our example of our love for one another here on Earth. God wants His people to be brought to Him. Work without ceasing to bring His people to Him. Remember to praise God's glory always in your life, and thank Him all day long while you live here on Earth. All glory to God our Creator and protector in life and forevermore, where in paradise our new selves created by Christ will abide.

22. New Selves Created by Christ

How should you love yourself? When we accept Christ into our hearts, He transforms us into a new person, who you cannot help but love, for His creation is perfect. However, your life experiences shape your old self, which Christ replaces with your new self. The old self is what we identify with if we are not careful. We think of it as who we are. It is familiar to us, and we think it safe because we know it. It is NOT safe.

The old self is where we keep our sinful nature. In it is all that which is displeasing to God—ego, envy, pride, selfishness, wrath, vengeance, unforgiveness, strife, uncaring attitudes toward others, anger, a hard heart, and the need to justify our unjust actions through argument.

The new self that Christ provides you is one filled with forgiveness, humility, desire for peace, awareness of the needs of others, being giving and caring, kindness, compassion, desire for unity with others, and a heart eager to forgive and to live in harmony with others.

Your old self can sometimes sneak out and affect your new self. The evil one is very good at telling us all, "Just be yourself," and if we listen, the old sinful self can make a brief appearance to our great detriment.

If you find yourself in a situation where you experience a negative reaction when speaking with another, it is a manifestation of the old self trying to infect your Christ-given new self, and you must ask yourself, "What is the new core sin that I am committing that I should react this way?" For it is the old self that you have allowed to taint your new self. The evil one is more clever than we are, and his lies can affect even the strongest believers if we do not pray Christ's protection from the evil one's lies on a daily basis.

Beware of falling into a sin cascade, one sin following another as your old self tries to assert itself. If you find yourself in that situation, stop what you are doing immediately and examine your heart to be aware of the sin you are committing and pray to Jesus for His protection against the lies of the evil one.

So, how you should love yourself is as Christ loves you, which is completely. If your question is how you should love your old self, it is not at all, for within that old self is all of your sin, and that sin leads to death. It is familiar to you, and you have been burdened all your life with a nature that keeps you separated from God. You need to abandon the old self completely; toss it aside like the filthy trash it is so that you can embrace the new self and praise Christ for giving you a new self that will conform with Christ's great and holy will.

Thank Christ specifically for each new attribute you have been given. "Thank you, Lord, for giving me kindness and compassion for others, for a forgiving heart, for a new desire for unity with my brothers and sisters, for replacing my ego with a loving heart, for replacing pride with compassion, for replacing wrath with love, for replacing vengeance with an eagerness to forgive, for self-justification with righteousness and a willingness to actually see and hear what is true. I love the new person I have been transformed into by you, my Lord; thank you, and keep me always in your sight and protect me from the assault of the evil one so that

I might fully become the new person you want me to become." Pray to Christ and thank Him for your transformation.

Every time we see our new, purer selves revealed, it is through praise to our Lord that we strengthen our new selves and banish our old selves from our lives.

23. Islam

The great shame of our current age is the division between Christians and the followers of Islam. The very name 'Islam' means submission to the will of God. Is that not what we followers of Christ seek also? But we tell ourselves they are wrong; they call God Allah instead of God. We must remember our Creator never identified Himself to us mere mortals with a name, only as I AM. Jesus called on His father and called Him Abba, which seems to be pretty close to what our Islamic brothers call our Father. Let us not nitpick over things that do not matter. We both are seeking to do God's will, which is what should be uniting Islam and Christianity. Since it is God's will that Christ is the means through which He brings seekers to Himself, then Christ will reach out to those seeking to do God's will and bring them to Him, as He has been promised by the Father that they are His.

The seeds of division have been sown between our Islamic brothers and sisters by evil men in our age whose intent is to create division between us in order to maintain their positions of status and privilege. There is money to be made through creating controversy and division, and evil men are only too happy to create that division and controversy to maintain their status and influence in this world, this is doing the work of the evil one. This is doing the work of the evil one both faiths are derived from the promise God made to Abraham, making us literally brothers and sisters in faith, as we both seek to do the will of God in this broken world.

We are natural allies, not enemies, as we also seek to do the will of God in this world. It is popular in certain segments of the media to call terrorists "Islamic terrorists." The term is meaningless because anyone who commits acts of terror in order to coerce others to a certain point of view has abandoned Islam and has turned his or her back on God. When people decide to use fear and intimidation to further their mistaken belief that they are doing God's will, they are going against God's will. It is never God's will to force us into love through fear. Such a thing is impossible. Fear is the opposite of love, and it is God's will that we seek His love out of our desire to seek Him.

There are terrorists in this broken world who would use fear to compel people to do as they deem proper. These men and women have all abandoned their faith and turned their backs on God. They do not follow Christ or Islam but follow the evil one, and having turned their backs on God, they will never experience paradise or the loving touch of God our Father, but instead will feel the touch of God's wrath.

Let us all stop creating divisions among ourselves by labeling terrorists with the name of Islam, because these men are not seeking to do the will of Allah, but have turned their back on Him and do not want to do His will. In the West we don't call the terrorists in our society "Christian terrorists" when they perform their horrendous deeds, even though many are working on a belief that somehow they are furthering God's desire. They also are just terrorists, neither Christian nor Islamic, for both sorts have turned their backs on God and will feel God's righteous wrath when the time of judgment arrives.

Let us all praise God our Father as we try to heal the divisions that evil men try to create among the children of Abraham. Pray to our Lord that the rift might be healed, so that, working together, we can bring God's harvest to Him. Time is short, and we need many more reapers if we are to have any chance of finishing God's task He has set before us. Let us all work together in harmony and peace to bring about God's will. Pray the Father heals and unites us together for His greater purpose in time to finish our given work.

24. Time

We as humans live in a universe where we can only experience the present, unlike God, who is outside of time. Time is something He created for us mortals to live within. We experience time only as "now." We cannot experience the future; we can remember the past, but we cannot relive it in any other sense than memory.

God gives us all an abundance of moments during which to give Him praise and glory. Every hour provides us with thirty-six hundred opportunities with which to thank our loving God and Creator for His abundant blessings and for drawing closer to Christ and asking Him to fill our soul with His living water so that we can draw even closer to God's abounding love.

Every day we have over eighty-six thousand moments during which we can be in communion with God our Creator. Yet, many people worry that they do not have enough time here on Earth. Such thinking misses the gift of time that God already provides us in abundance. If eighty-six thousand moments a day is not enough, how much more time do you need?

We worry about the future, which is an illusion, because we cannot experience the future, nor can we change the past. We only have now, and God provides us with more than enough now with which to sing praise to our Lord, to seek communion with Christ, and to seek to do God's holy will.

Do any of us really use all the time God has already given us to always be in His holy presence? We become distracted by the cares of this earthly life and fail to properly use the gift of time God has given us. We fail to be always in prayer and rejoicing to our Lord.

25. Connecting Our Souls to Our Lord

As is His desire for us, most people cannot even muster one hour of proper prayer and thankfulness to the Lord during the day, let alone the eighty-six thousand moments of true connection to the Lord that He is seeking from us. If we find it so difficult to reach God in every moment of our lives, it is surely due to lack of practice. We must develop the habit of thankfulness, always, and for the habit to develop, we must make a conscious effort to reinforce it.

Christ will provide His strength and support for us weak mortals as we seek to develop our good habits. He will fill our souls with His living waters continuously, making our soul always connected to God, singing His praise, and causing our heart and mind to follow suit, always in worship and thankfulness to our Creator. When fully developed, your soul will fill your heart and mind with God's praises so that you can actually live each moment as God intended.

God, our Creator, has given us all more than ample time with which to become connected to Him. Live each moment as the precious gift that it is, and you will find more joy and peace in your life than you ever expected, for each moment is a separate gift from our loving Father. Enjoy His gift always, as it is His desire that we savor this life and use our time wisely and with purpose.

26. Leading a Life of Intent

Praise God, Father and Creator of our lives, which we can use to glorify and exalt Him always. Do not live a careless life, but live with focus and intent, the focus always to please our Creator, and the intent to do the good works God has given us to perform here on Earth. With a conscious effort of will, we can focus our hearts upon God hundreds, if not thousands, of times daily.

The practice of being always ready to thank God and praise Him requires us to develop new habits and will be difficult at times. As the world's cares intrude into our lives, we must, with constant practice of joyful praise, expressions of love for God, and thankfulness for the great blessings He is constantly giving, overcome our temptation to let the world interfere with our communication with God.

We develop a bond with God so that our souls, which will dwell directly in the presence of God, fill our hearts and minds with constant assurance of God's love and strength. We will reach a point in our lives where we will no longer have to rely on faith, because our soul will dwell directly with our Father and will know for a fact that He is with us. Our souls will burn with God's holy fire, which will purge all doubt and give us peace and strength to cope with any worldly problems we encounter.

We live in a corrupted world, and there are problems. God did not promise we would not have reasons to be afraid in this life. The way to overcome fear in this life is the practice of drawing near to our Creator, through leading a life focused upon God and developing the true bond between God and your soul.

Practice every second God gives you so that your soul is in constant communion with our Lord. We overcome our fear at that time because we will know for a fact that God is in control of our lives, and we know He gives us the strength to overcome any hardship.

God wants our souls to be dwelling directly in His presence; we need to practice the habits that will draw us into God's holy presence so that we achieve God's desire for constant communion of our souls with Him. Do not fear for anything. God's will is sure to be done here on Earth as in heaven; since it is already destined to happen, God's will is the only possible outcome.

God wills it, so it will happen. Trust in the Lord; strengthen the bond between your soul and God, and all your fear and doubt will vanish like the morning dew because you will know God directly and know His all-encompassing love. When your soul shares with what your heart and mind knows, you will be directly connected to God at all times.

27. Work

We live in a world where God wants us to work with our hands and seek out a modest and humble life. So, seek to work as God instructs us, but do not work for the sake of work only. Let every aspect of your work be a praise to the Lord, and always do your utmost to perform your work in a manner that gives glory to God.

We are here on Earth to be servants to each other, so let your work be a service to your fellows, but also a blessing, which is pleasing to God. Even the most menial task can be both a service and a moment to thank God for the chance to be a servant in this life. Always thank God for the opportunities He gives us to be servants for our fellows. Jesus, while teaching us His perfect Word during His time on Earth, makes clear that being a servant should be our goal in life and especially with our work, which should always be in a spirit of servanthood and at the same time an act of praise to our Father and Lord.

There is no such thing as a job to perform that is too small not to do the absolute best we can. God charges us to make our work a praise to Him and to try to always view work as an act of exultation for our Father. Thanks be to God for the chance to be servants in the service of our Lord and Father for the easing of the world's burdens and cares for our fellows during our life journey here on Earth.

It is important that while you do the work God calls you to do, you remain in contact with God, asking Him to accept your work as you praise Him and thank Him for the chance to be a servant. Draw ever closer to God through the constant practice of thankful servanthood. Every moment you spend doing God's mission allows you to reflect upon God's divine plan for humanity and the part you play to make this world a better place for all through your labors.

Thanks be to our Father always and to His Son, who directs our path to the Father. We unfortunately live in a culture that does not value the idea of servanthood and work, nor modest and humble lives as something to seek after.

28. Culture of Excess

Ours is a culture in which extravagant excess is celebrated as being part of the good life. The cultural icons that the majority of people look up to are, for the most part, shallow people, living lives of overconsumption and excess. Even those who should be living as examples of restraint and humility are fully living the life of extravagant excess.

Self-proclaimed leaders in the teaching of our Lord's Word take the contributions of their followers, which are intended to spread the Word of our Lord to all the nations. Instead, these contributions are being spent on mansions for the "teacher," extravagant cars, and even aircraft. This all must be most obscene in the eyes of our Father in heaven, but it reflects the capture by our culture of excess even of those who should best know the danger. If the self-proclaimed leaders of the Christian movement can be so easily captured by this culture, it is clearly a very effective way that the evil one uses to separate us from God.

Greed and avarice are part of our nature prior to Christ's giving us our new selves, and our old sinful nature can reemerge into our lives if we are not ever-vigilant and always in prayer for protection. We must be diligent in our efforts to shun the culture we live in. Take care of what media you consume in your home, lest you become captured. The lifestyles of the rich and famous should be to all followers of Christ a warning of how not to live and an example of how our sinful, selfish nature can lead us down a path that turns worldly wealth and worldly pleasure into false gods.

God provides us with all we need in life, but once we become captured by greed and addicted to this world's pleasures, having our needs met somehow becomes not enough for us. We want God to also provide our wants for us. In His mercy, God does not grant our wants, because our wants are based on our sinful nature and are contrary to the way God chooses for us to live. Our wants are based on sins, greed, excess pleasure, avarice, selfishness, envy, and ego. We fall into sin when we start to imagine ourselves living a life filled with excess, a life of pointless ease and sloth, given over to pleasure and indolence.

In His mercy, God does not curse us if we become captured by this desire to be consumed by consumerism, but He keeps most of us grounded in reality, making us live within our God-given provisioning. It is up to us to always thank God for what He has provided in His mercy and love for us.

Turn off the TV. It is the tool the evil one uses to tempt the chosen into losing sight of God's path and creating within even the strongest a desire to live lives of glamor and fame, as if either has ever saved even one person's soul. Be content with the gifts God has already given you, and let the only fame you seek be that of your eternal salvation. If you seek the rewards of the earth, you will forgo the rewards that God has prepared for you to enjoy in eternity. Choose carefully what it is you really desire—earthly corrupted rewards or the pure, clean, and holy rewards God prepares for us. It is our greedy, sinful natures that make it necessary that we have Christ for our intercession.

29. Why Christ?

When God created man, He gave us free will to make decisions affecting our relationship with Him. God made man and placed us in Eden, at which point man chose to be disobedient to God and severed the intimate relationship that we shared with God at that time. God, in His mercy, gave man a second chance to restore the relationship, unlike the angels who rebelled against Him, whom He cast down into Hell.

God's decision was to send mankind a Messiah who could restore the one-on-one relationship between God and man. God decreed to Moses that Israel sacrifice perfect animals for the sins of the people. Mere animals can in no way be perfect enough for God, which is why we need Christ as our intermediary. Only He is perfect enough to satisfy God's desire for a pure and perfect lamb of God, worthy and clean enough to be our sin sacrifice for man's turning from God in the beginning.

God chose Jesus as His son, and Jesus accepted His role as sin sacrifice for mankind, knowing full well that we did not deserve His great sacrifice for us all, because He chose to save us while we were all still sinners and steeped in evil, yet He still showed us His great love and compassion and accepted His assignment from God, knowing full well the ordeal that He would have to undergo after His ministry here on Earth.

It is beyond our human understanding the amount of love Jesus showed us with His willingness to sacrifice Himself for us while we were still sinners, using our free will to continue to oppose God's will. When man fell, God set forth the rules that mankind would now have to live by within this world.

God let the evil one loose in the world only after mankind rebelled, and we can reduce his influence on Earth through obedience to the Word. The evil one is still interfering with our relationship with God. It is only through Christ's death and resurrection that we are made clean in God's eyes. The one final pure and perfect sacrifice has been completed as God willed it from the beginning, and we now can be washed white and pure through the blood of Christ.

Who chose to be our Savior? All praise to our Lord always. "Jesus loves me, this I know, because the Bible tells me so, as does my soul." Thank Him often for His sacrifice for our collective sin, and ask His intercession for each time you sin again, and you will be forgiven for your transgressions when you repent directly to Christ Jesus and ask Him to act as your shield against the evil one and ask for forgiveness for your failures.

30. The New Covenant

When we accept Christ at baptism as our Lord and Savior, He provides us with a new, better self and gives us a new covenant that supplants the old covenant given to Moses by God for the people of Israel.

Too many who call themselves Christians today are mired in the old covenant and the law. If they want to live under the law, perhaps they should become Jewish, since the law was given to Moses for the nation of Israel. The new covenant with Christ has fulfilled the old, but all too many Christians cling to the law as a weapon to assail nonbelievers with their sin. These people seem to not grasp that to live under the law is to assure failure to achieve salvation, forgetting that nothing man can do on his own is good enough or pure enough to ever satisfy God's standard of perfection, and His standard already exists in the person of Jesus, upon whom the new covenant is based.

It is through Christ's direct intercession and the offer of the Holy Spirit that we now have any hope of salvation and eternal life with God. The new covenant is based on love of Christ and His love of us, and it is spirit-based and not law-based. So, it must be practiced in spirit between our souls and Christ Jesus on a daily basis, during our frequent prayers of thanksgiving and praise to our Lord God.

Expecting anyone to live under the law to satisfy God is to condemn that person, as no one can possibly achieve the perfection required to meet God's standards through his or her own efforts. Christians should understand this and stop trying to get nonbelievers to live to a standard they themselves cannot achieve. Such attitudes work to drive the nonbelievers away from Christ, who rightly sees the people touting these ideas as being hypocrites themselves. These false teachers are not to be trusted and are not true messengers of our Lord and His true love and true Word. And, as such, they act to separate God from those He is seeking, predisposing the call to not trust because of the false witness some have provided them in the name of Christ.

Be true lights to the world. Let the true and pure light of Christ's love shine out from you, and you will reflect Christ's true love for all of His people. Be a beacon of hope and light to the entire world by letting Christ's pure light and love of the new covenant shine through so that people can learn to worship our Creator in spirit and love and become baptized into the true faith.

31. Baptism

When we are baptized, we undergo a transformation where our old sinful selves share in the death of Jesus on the cross and are put to death, and in the place of the old sinful self, Christ creates a new righteous self for us, which shares in the resurrection and eternal life Jesus bought for us and also becomes an abode for the Holy Spirit who then dwells within us.

Some wonder if it is proper to baptize infants. It is proper, because infants also share mankind's sinful nature at birth and need the new, pure self that Christ provides upon baptism. The infants also need the help of the Holy Spirit, who will direct the children as they grow and mature, giving guidance and direction, assisting parents in their children's spiritual journey until they become born again.

32. Born Again

Jesus tells us we must all be born again in spirit and faith. With baptism, Christ replaces our old sinful self with a new self that is filled with all the attributes that God finds pleasing, and we become filled with the Holy Spirit.

To be born again is a more active phase for believers. We must actively and aggressively seek out an intimate, personal relationship with our Lord Jesus, being in constant prayer, thanksgiving, supplication, and worship in order to forge a bond of faith that feeds our souls and allows us to dwell in God's holy presence at all times. Our soul knows God's love for us from being in His presence, and with that knowledge, has assurance that God loves us and has all our needs met now and for the future, leaving us reborn into an assurance of salvation. Part of the process of becoming born again is always seeking out God's Word.

33. Being In the Word

In the beginning was the Word, and He was with God, and He was God. Being in the Word is beyond just reading the Bible daily, although that is certainly important. Being WITH the Word is preferred.

When you start your devotional, ask Christ to draw close, and you can actually feel Him draw near to you, a feeling of calm and joy that feeds your soul and will bring you joy. When reading or listening to your Bible, be with the Word. If you have any questions, ask Him directly, and He will answer you. He, who is God, tells us directly what God finds most pleasing from us mortals and gives us clear directions on how we should comport ourselves here on Earth.

By being in Christ's presence daily by our request and our direct pursuit of His true Word, we bolster our spirit and feed our soul and further our quest to be born again in faith and spirit as directed by Jesus. We can look forward to that day with joy and anticipation when we will all be directly touched by God as Jesus takes our hands and leads us from this world to our new and better home, created in the beginning by our Creator. God created both this universe and heaven.

34. Reconciling Science with the Bible

Fear of the Lord is the beginning of wisdom. This is most certainly true; once we realize just how vast and powerful our Creator is, we cannot help but feel a fearful wonder when we contemplate His vast and limitless powers.

When trying to reconcile science with the Bible, we need to ask ourselves two questions. The first being, can man discover anything that God wants to remain hidden? The answer is of course not. The second question to ask is, is it in God's nature to deceive? The answer to this question is no.

God's nature is light and truth. So, it stands to reason that anything He allows science to discover about the nature of His creation, that discovery is true because God Himself allowed us to discover the information. The Bible tells us in Genesis 1:3 that God created everything by calling forth "let there be light," which is the most succinct explanation that I've ever heard of the big bang that started the physical universe.

At the same time God created the physical universe, He created the heavens and all of our souls, along with everything else in heaven. God not only created everything with one act of will; He planned everything that was ever going to happen and set up the physical rules governing how the universe operated, as well as how life, once started, would operate within the universe.

To ignore science or to discount it as anti-Biblical would be giving God far less awe and respect than He deserves. This isn't a God who waves His hand, and everything is finished. He is a creator who created everything with His Word and set up how everything was going to work, all the physical operations of an entire physical universe, and set in motion His plan for mankind's salvation even before there was a mankind to save.

Mere mortals cannot even begin to conceive of the amount of power God possesses in order to have done what He so clearly has done, and it is science that points us to His unimaginable power. So, it is science that reinforces the Bible's account of God's creation. Everywhere, God leaves clues for science to see how great His scope and how far-reaching His power is. Understanding the scale of God's creation should inspire awe and some fear in us, for God is truly far above us. And the fact that He created us out of love and wants us with Him for eternity should fill us with joy and awesome wonder in our every waking moment.

35. Biblical History

Does science provide evidence of biblical events? It turns out, yes. There is evidence that the story of the flood recounts an actual event, and there is physical evidence to back up biblical history.

In the Indian Ocean, off the coast of Madagascar, in twelve thousand feet of water, is a site named Burckle Crater, left over from a comet or asteroid impact from around the time of Noah's flood. The impact in such a deep portion of the ocean would have caused gigatons of water vapor to be released into the atmosphere, making it rain for months on end. Since it is such a deep ocean, the tsunami released would have been enormous, flooding all coastal regions in the Indian Ocean basin, including the Persian Gulf. It would have seemed as if the very wells of the earth had opened up to anyone around to experience the event. The ocean would have flooded far inland, and the rain would not have ceased falling for months at a time, forty days and forty nights at least. The entire valley of the Tigris and Euphrates would have become a vast inland sea.

God warned Noah about the coming disaster in time for Noah to save his family and livestock, when all around him perished in the flood. Eventually, Noah and his family drifted upon the new sea until they reached high ground, and thus God saved the line of David and of Jesus.

God uses nature in His miracles. Just because something is natural doesn't mean it is not a miracle. God intervened directly to achieve His purpose here on Earth, and He is still active and will act in our lives in a direct way if we are open to hearing Him speaking to us when He calls us. Because God is in control of nature, He uses nature for His purposes.

36. Rely on Christ

There is no need for us here on Earth to have all the answers. We have the solution for all of our problems readily available for the asking; we merely must humble ourselves and ask for help. For some, this is a difficult thing, admitting that we are not the masters of our destiny, that we are not in charge or in control. We must let Christ know that we accept His will in our lives and His control over our lives in order to enjoy the peace and joy that He intends for us to have when we accept His will and His preordained plan for our lives. God loves humble hearts that accept His will and direction in their lives. We need to release our old selves in order to live as our new selves.

37. Take Up Your Cross and Follow Christ

When we take up our cross and follow Christ, it is an act of giving up our old sinful self to join Christ on the cross to be put to death alongside Him so that our newly created and worthy self can join in the resurrection provided by Jesus. Our old sinful nature must die alongside Jesus. If we are ever to die to sin to join in the resurrection with Christ, we must humble ourselves before Christ and ask that He put to death the old selfish self and help build up the new selfless self He has given us at baptism so that we can follow His plan for us without resistance from our old sinful selves.

Humility is essential in order to maintain a proper relationship with God. He is far above us in goodness, power, and intent, and we must be humble in submitting to His much greater plans for us. We must all surrender our will to that of God.

38. Surrender Our Will to That of God

If you are a person who feels the need to be in control all the time, you need to go directly to Christ and surrender your will to that of God. Ask forgiveness for not trusting in God's plan for you, and ask forgiveness for your lack of faith in God's provisioning for you. You must make your act of surrender an overt act of faith and devotion directly with Christ, and of course, mean it. We are all here as God's instruments.

39. Be God's Tool on Earth

We are all sent here to live our lives on Earth with a purpose, that purpose being to be a support and help for every other person on the planet. We must be active in our purpose in order to be effective; a tool that isn't being used is not useful. Be a spirit-filled tool whose works flow out for all to see. The power for our tool is the love of Christ Jesus. Let His love guide your path and be your power as you work to gather His harvest. Each tool has its own purpose.

40. Seek Out Your Purpose

The key to finding your purpose is simply asking Christ to guide your path and to use you to do His will. Pray, "Your will be done, Lord. Free me from my self-interest. Make me a pure instrument of your will, Lord, worthy of the work you have for me. Forgive me for my failure to follow your directions in the past; please guide me in the true path you have set forth for me. How do I feed your sheep, Lord?"

41. Feed My Sheep

After the resurrection, Jesus asked Peter three times if he loved Him. In John 21:15–19, we read that Peter was hurt and answered, "Yes, my Lord. You know all things, and you know that I love you." Jesus answered Peter, "Then feed my sheep."

Jesus said this to Peter not to remind him of his three denials, but to make the point to actually physically make sure that Jesus's sheep were fed. A starving person will not hear the message to feed the spiritual needs of His sheep, send people to reach His sheep, and be part of a body of believers who support missions to other nations so that all the nations are reached before the end comes. Jesus also told Peter to feed His sheep emotionally by assuring everyone that they are indeed worthy of salvation and that Christ wants them because He has been promised them by the Father.

We need to stop telling those we don't like that they aren't worthy, because that just isn't true any more than the fact that any of us are worthy of salvation when you get down to the truth of it. So, stop being selective in your condemnation, and welcome everyone as Christ welcomes everyone.

42. Shaken, Not Stirred

The easiest thing in life is to get to a place where complacency sets in, that place where things are going along pretty well and you haven't examined your life in a while and all seems okay. I know. I was there for decades before I took a hard look and decided I really didn't like the person I had become, cold and uncaring, selfish, arrogant, argumentative, and always having to be right.

Upon reading my Bible, I had to ask myself, was I doing what Jesus was instructing me to do in Matthew 5 and 25? I had to answer truthfully, no, I was not.

I was shaken to my core. I want to be on Christ's right hand on the final day, and I was stirred to make some fundamental changes to my attitudes and my daily activities and interactions. It is my hope that anyone reading these pages will make similar reflections, and if shaken with a realization of shortcomings, will not fail to be stirred to make changes in their life that will be pleasing to God our Father.

43. Understanding God's Heart and Mind

We spend a lot of time reading the Bible and memorizing chapter and verse citations without really understanding exactly what it is that God is telling us. This is why it is important to ask the Word to be with you when you are in the Word. He will come when asked, and when He is present, if you have any questions about what you have read, you can go directly to the one true teacher for the answer, and He will answer all your questions.

It works. I have been asking questions for years, and He always leads me to answers. Not always the ones I expect, but He does answer the questions; you just have to ask with true intent, and He will respond with truth.

To ask questions of our Lord is not to show a lack of faith, but it is showing Him we are trying to love Him with all of our mind, all of our heart, and all of our soul, as we are directed in the greatest commandment. (Matthew 22:37.) So, give your mind over to God, and spend some serious time asking Him hard questions. He will not be offended but will view it as worship time where you show you trust Him to show you truths that enable you to better understand your Creator in all His majesty and power.

When reading and memorizing your Bible, have the Word with you by asking Him to be by your side while doing the activity and ask Him to help you understand the context of what you are reading or memorizing; as in so much of the Bible, context is everything. Having Him explain the context will help you better understand God's heart and mind on the subject.

Don't rely on any earthly teacher or preacher to tell you, when you have the one true teacher available for the asking. Jesus will come and sit with you for the asking and will answer all your questions, and your understanding and love of God will grow as a result. Start the process sooner rather than later because this life is fleeting, as are we all.

44. Jars of Clay

We all are destined to live forever once we embrace the salvation offered through Christ. But the earthly vessels we inhabit are like jars of clay, as referenced numerous times throughout the Bible. Genesis 3:19 says, "From dust we are, and to dust will return."

Our bodies are fragile and were never intended to be our permanent home, just a temporary abode to occupy while here on Earth, prone to disease, hunger, and accident. If you feel the need to change direction in your life or take up a new vocation of service, the sooner the better, because none of us know how long our fragile jars of clay are going to last. Only the potter knows how many days any of us has left, so we need to act as if all of our days are numbered, and the number is not that high. Godspeed in your quest, and with the help of Christ, you will not fail. Our highest aspiration should be to become servants.

45. Be a Servant

The greatest thing that we can aspire to be is a servant to others. According to Jesus, the first step in becoming a servant is to don the new attribute of humility that Christ gives us in our new selves at baptism.

Humility is definitely a learned trait for most of us, as it is not a trait cherished in our society. To be humble is to assume the needs of the other person outweigh our own. Let that car line jump; it might be later than you. It will cost you nothing but a bit of pride to let those people in.

So, learn humility, and your blood pressure will probably drop as a result. Pride goes before the fall, but humility brings contentment and happiness. Your life will improve vastly if you are able to become a humble person among others and before Christ. You become happier, and those around you are also happier. It's a big ask, and goes against our nature, but it is among the attributes Christ gives us at baptism. We just need to nurture it so that it grows. And with humility you will have few regrets.

46. Regrets

Now is not the time for regrets; now is the time to resolve any lingering issues in your life while there is still time, so act while you can if it is possible. And, if not, you can always reconcile in heaven, where we will all have perfect understanding, being covered by the love of the Lord. Try not to let one of those regrets be a failure to reach out to another person to share the gospel. If so, you still have time to try. Christ takes note of our efforts and will judge us on our efforts to lead a worthy life.

47. A Blessed Life

Your goal should be to live a life filled with service to others, dedicated to making this life the best possible for everyone here on Earth, with the aim of increasing social justice for everyone and economic equality for all. These two areas will fix 90 percent of what ails this hurting world. We need to become true emissaries for Christ and work to make this world more like He wants it to be.

In view of the latest events happening in our world, the global pandemic, the effects of climate change, social unrest, and creeping political changes toward dictatorship, it seems like this world might just be winding down, and we do not have a lot of time to fix our problems. Our only hope is to be in constant prayer to our Lord and to actively choose to be agents of change in our world. When we act collectively to bring about changes of leadership to make the country more perfectly reflect the will of the Lord for a fair and equitable nation, working for the common good of all the people, providing the basic needs for everyone, then at least we will be better placed to face the coming trials.

For myself, I do not know how much longer I have to act, but I recognize that my options are limited pretty much to trying to get my life in order and myself in a better relationship with God, and lots of prayer for the world situation. We are all dependent upon the mercy of our Lord to get us through the tests of this world, of which there will undoubtedly be many. The Lord walks among us; do not forget to ask so that you can receive. He will give us all strength and His protection. So, pray hard, and work hard to make the world the refuge for all of God's people, wherever they are

The time to harvest is upon us, so we must redouble our efforts to make the outreach to reach the lost and those that Christ wants to be brought to Him. We need to get out of Christ's way in reaching His people by stopping our labeling of people and groups so that we don't drive away the very people Christ wants brought to Him.

In hopeful prayer to our Lord and Creator always, I pray the peace and hope of the Lord come to everyone, and we can all be agents of God here on Earth and bring glory and honor to His holy name always. I also pray for Jesus to strengthen my faith in His ability to guide the world through the coming trials, to help me stop worrying about things He is taking care of. He has us all in His hands, so we have no need for worry.

Epilogue

When we look around us today, we appear to be surrounded by chaos and troubles without end. Staying strong in our faith and hope in Christ can be difficult, which makes prayer even more important. Pray that Christ continues to look after us and that He grants us wisdom so we can take what steps we need in order to do our part in making the earth better for all who live here.

With Christ's help, we can transform our country into a fair and equal society, allowing us to reach all those people that Christ wants us to reach. Pray that we all become a light unto the world, shining God's love everywhere we go. In Christ, we are assured salvation. It's our duty to help reach those people who need to hear the Word of our Lord and Savior so that they also share in Christ's redemptive love.

We need to be careful of the face we show the world, which sometimes sees Christians as people with mouthfuls of scripture and hearts full of hate. Remember Paul's exhortation in Ephesians 4:29 to only say those things that are true and are uplifting and build up the faith of others. Our approach should be one of gentleness and loving kindness, so that those we meet will see Christ's image in our every outward appearance. So that those we meet will want to have the peace and serenity in the face of problems that we will be able to display to the world, knowing that our salvation is assured through Christ and that we can withstand any trial with the help of Jesus.

So, pray for strength of faith so that in times of stress and need, we show the world our faith and hope in Christ. The fate of the world is in God's hands, and we must always remember that the woes and chaos that we see are part of God's grand plan for His creation and stay strong in our faith in God's plans and protection.

When things are looking bleak, also reach out to your fellow Christians so that you bolster each other in faith, and in doing so, you will both find it easier to stay strong in your faith. By working together as a body, we can overcome our trials and emerge from them stronger due to the shared experience of beseeching Christ for His intercession and help.

God is in control of everything; we just have to hold onto our faith and reliance on Him to take care of us, whatever the future has in store for us. We belong to Jesus through baptism, and He will stand with us in all situations, so long as we keep faith and retain our reliance on Him. Christ stands with us so long as we abide in Him. Praise Christ for His protective presence always. We are His, and He is ours for eternity. Praise and thankfulness to His glorious name, always and forever.

Fear not. You are under the protection of an ever-present God who has you in His hands and who loves you as His own child. His protection will not fail; His protection cannot fail. He is God, and it is His will that controls the heavens and Earth. He is omnipotent, omnipresent, and atemporal, which means He knows everything that ever happened and knows everything about what is to come. Everything that happens is known to Him, and He is in control of it all. So, we need fear nothing. He has it covered. As God, He has already seen and directed the end times. He sees all and knows all and has the situation firmly under control.

Lean on Christ for strength when needed; He will not fail you. Also stay in communion with other brothers and sisters in Christ so that we can be a source of strength for each other. We are not alone in our troubles. We can lean on each other, and we always have the strength of Jesus if needed. We need to always remember who is in control. And our worries will shrink to a manageable size.

Have faith in the protection and provisioning of the Lord. He will not let you down. He is the light that will never dim. His is the well that will never run dry, and He is the true bread that gives life in abundance and which will never cease to give us life. He is the solid foundation that we can build our faith on and will always be there for us whenever we need it, rock solid and enduring. Knowing God's invincibility gives us a source of strength that we can always lean on. God will not fail us so long as we keep Him in focus.

The trying times we are in can be viewed as an opportunity God has given us to better prepare ourselves for the final judgment, as described in Mathew 25. We have a chance to feed the hungry, give drink to the thirsty, provide shelter for those in need, clothe the naked, take care of the sick, welcome the stranger, and give help to all who need it. God has given us a chance to rectify any shortcomings we have in our lives in these areas that He is going to judge us on so that we will be numbered among the sheep, not the goats, on the day of judgment.

I pray we each examine our heart and ask Christ to show us, each and every one, what steps we need to take to become the person that Christ would have us become. God grants us time to work for His desire. He has given us plenty of advance warning that the earth is winding down. Through the loving kindness of Jesus, we can all act in accordance with Jesus's desire that we take care of everyone left here on Earth. The time draws near, but we still have time to change our priorities and follow the example of Christ on how to care for our fellows.

The path to Christ can be difficult. Jesus Himself tells us this in the Bible. But any other path we might choose leads to oblivion and death. Pray earnestly to Jesus to show you the way He would have you take so that you, too, can enjoy the reward He promises us for our obedience to His instructions. Keep your eyes on the visage of Christ, and you will not fail in keeping to His path to salvation. These things I know are true.

God made us and protects us. Christ Jesus is the promised Messiah, who makes it possible to draw near to God, that, as God's son Jesus through His sacrifice, makes it possible for us mere mortals to be actual children of God, and that God the Father is good beyond any mortal understanding. God's love for His children is boundless.

This I know as a fact because I've actually experienced His touch of peace and love, and I cannot describe with mere words how powerful His love is and how powerful His protection is for us. I know that at the end of this life, we will be brought up to paradise by Jesus, and it is going to be better than any of us dared dream. No pain, no sorrow or troubles, just endless joy and peace in the presence of our Lord Christ Jesus. I know that Jesus walks among us and is available to us by simply asking Him for His intercession. I know that at that time we will be joined by those who passed before us and that we will have perfect understanding of each other so that any strife we experienced on Earth will be resolved through the perfect love of Christ Jesus.

As we wait for the coming of Christ, we still have to live in this world and strive to make it a better place for all. There are five words that will go far in making this world better for everyone. They are: "How can I (WE) help you?" If we practice trying to actively make the world better for everyone, we can approach Jesus on that final day in the assurance that we were good and faithful servants to Him and we fulfilled His command to love one another and to treat everyone else as we would want to be treated.

It is a huge job that we as individuals cannot hope to achieve. We must join together as a civil society or as church bodies to pool our resources in order to be effective. Together, we are strong, and we have the resources of heaven for the asking. Christ Jesus will answer our prayers.

No matter what is going on in your life, never stop seeking God's light. Jesus is the light of the world, and He wants you to seek Him out and become a child of God. Just ask for Him to come to you, and He will.

God created us to have eternal life with Him in paradise, and His mechanism to bring that about is to have us follow Christ Jesus by accepting Him as our Lord and Savior. Jesus will show us His love for the asking. We, on our own, can never lead a perfect life; it is through Jesus that we are perfected and made worthy to be called children of God.

Do not delay in seeking out Christ, for in His loving embrace, we can let go of our earthly problems and come to peace here on Earth.